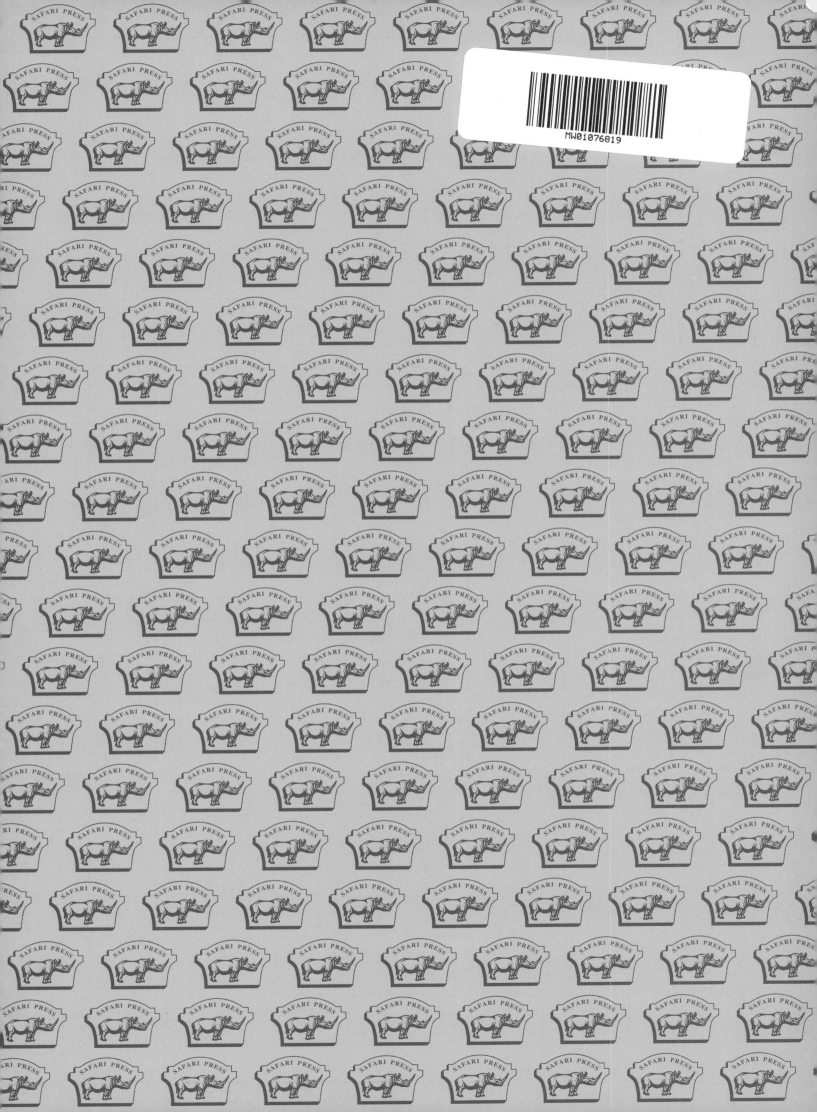

Great Hunters

Their trophy rooms & collections

Safari Press Inc.

PACKNOWLEDGMENT OF HOTOGRAPHERS

1. Anderson, Dennis & Leean/Dennis Davis Photography
2. Cabela, Dick & Mary/Michael Ives NRA & David Cabela
3. Chateau de Gien/B. Voisin—CDT Loiret 2007
4. D'Aoust, Georges/Gordon King Photography
5. Dickson, Mark/John Watkins Photography
6. Gomez Sequeira, Dr. Marcial/Julio Lozano
7. Kauffman, John/Photography by Kelli Trontel
8. Knap, Jerome & Halina/John T. Fowler
9. Maki, Alan/W. Garth Dowling Photography
10. Minx, Brook F./Don Glentzer and George Gutenburg
11. Musée de la Chasse et de la Nature/Erwan Le Marchand, Luc Boelgly or DR
12. Revelle, Jack (Joyce)/Tarolli Studio
13. Simpson, Mike/Bill Honza
14. Stromberg, Doug/Bob Deveny
15. Williamson, Gregory/Jeremy Enlow with Steelshutter Photography
16. Wulff, Günter/Albert Meyer

The trademark Safari Press ® is registered with the U.S. Patent and Trademark Office and with government trademark and patent offices in other countries.

First edition

Safari Press

2013, Long Beach, California

ISBN 978-1-57157-428-2

Library of Congress Catalog Card Number: 97067705

10 9 8 7 6 5 4 3 2 1

Printed in China

Readers wishing to receive the Safari Press catalog, featuring many fine books on big-game hunting, wingshooting, and sporting firearms, should write to Safari Press, P.O. Box 3095, Long Beach, CA 90803, USA. Tel: (714) 894-9080 or visit our Web site at www.safaripress.com.

TABLE OF CONTENTS

Hunters listed alphabetically

THE SHARING OF GREAT HUNTERS

Trophy rooms are magical. Big-game hunters are unique world travelers and explorers, for they experience the earth's most remote places and visit people who may never have seen an outsider. Unlike most tourists, they are the paramount collectors. They not only bring back the wildlife specimens they get, but most frequently they gather artifacts from their safaris to exotic locales. Why do they collect all this? Simply to share.

These adventurers use their memorabilia to reminisce, but they also use them to show others many things that would be impossible for them to see otherwise. Hunters are generous to showcase their world travels, which they do by sharing their trophy rooms. These hunter-conservationists are representative of the hunting fraternity; they teach that wildlife worldwide must have an economic value to be sustainable. Conservation is the wise sustainable use of the renewable resource of wildlife, which can be achieved through a well-managed hunting program, and educating those who share the habitat is paramount. The message must be that wildlife has value and is worth protecting, and this forms the basis of the ecological, economical, and sociopolitical pillars of sustainability.

Trophy rooms come in many forms—a modest den, one or more rooms in the house, a separate trophy house, a restaurant, a business showplace, special homes in which the residents share each room with their collectibles, and museums. Big or small, the wildlife specimens are normally accompanied by native arts/crafts, bronzes, and fine art. These *Great Hunters* volumes are a unique collection of such thoughtful sportspersons who share their memorabilia with the rest of us. Here are a few examples of some who went "over the top" to go beyond the mere sharing.

Dick and Mary Cabela's idea for their new elaborate home went far beyond the ordinary. Their design was inspired with a look to the future, for once they are gone, their trophy rooms/house will become a federally registered museum. They have an interactive video with sound effects that bring the outdoors inside with sunsets and shooting stars, sounds of the wild, thunderstorms, and much more. At the present they are working with schools, Scouts, and child-based groups, and they often donate tours to be auctioned off for charity events.

Renee and Paul Snider for years have had a similar interactive exhibit in their Elk Grove, California, home. Look at a view of the world's mountains, forests, and savannas as you peruse the pages of their section of this book. The Sniders host many charitable events, including the River Oak Center for Children, as well as fundraisers for SCI and the NRA (once years ago with Charlton Heston). They have had over three thousand visitors annually, and for twenty years that has included Scouts, church groups, and needy children.

Carl Ross, of hunting- and golf-business fame, developed the Safari Business Park on Dean Martin Way just south of the Las Vegas Strip. The outside of the six-block complex is adorned with double-size giraffe and elephant bronze appliqués. The Safari Park office is Carl's "trophy room" and is a federally recognized museum known as the Safari Learning Center. The leopard print carpet accessorizes his showroom, and the adjoining office houses extraordinary wildlife bronzes and paintings. A huge room houses around two hundred mounted specimens from a life-size giraffe on down. The complex encourages tours for schools, Scouts, and churches, as well as a meeting place for clubs. In fact, the directors and past recipients of the Weatherby Award Foundation utilized the facility for their prebanquet cocktail party in January 2012.

Whether big or small, private or public, the trophy room and its creators are eager to share—be it to entertain, educate, or to spread the message of wildlife conservation to all.

Chris Klineburger
Author of *Gamemasters of the World: A Chronicle of Sport Hunting and Conservation*

ANDERSON

I'm one of those rare hunters who without any youth mentoring became a world-class hunter. It was *In the Blood* for me. I began my hunting career by going after deer and small game in my early teens, and then I took up varmint calling. It was not long before I had accumulated the "100 Club" trophy for recorded predator takes.

As my business and family responsibilities grew and required more attention, I put hunting on the shelf for some time. My wife, Leean, and I founded and continue to operate one of the largest seafood processing and distribution companies in Southern California. But hunting was never far from my mind.

After a hiatus of some years, I resumed big-game hunting in the late '80s. It was then that I was invited to attend a local Safari Club International chapter meeting, and it became obvious to me that I wanted to become involved. There was not only the camaraderie but the volunteer work of SCI that appealed to me.

I became committed to the mission of Safari Club International, and after several years I rose to a leadership role. I served as president of Safari Club International in 2007–2008. I dedicated myself to the mission of recruiting young hunters into the hunting community, and to that end I founded the Youth Safari Day outreach program. We began the program in 1998, and each year we reach approximately three thousand young people in Southern California; the number continues to grow each year. I was awarded the highest honor from Safari Club International for my volunteer work, receiving the SCI Hall of Fame award.

I have also volunteered for and committed to SCI's Hunter Legacy Fund endowment, and I am a board member of the Weatherby Foundation and the Conklin Foundation. I'm a life member of SCI, Grand Slam Club/Ovis, the Wild Sheep Foundation, the NRA, and the Boone and Crockett Club.

I have been able to divide my time between hunting and volunteer commitments, and both have been rewarding. I have hunted on six continents from the highest mountains to the lowest desert. I have been able to complete the SCI's World Hunting Award and the Ovis's Triple Slam. I have collected well over two hundred species, which are displayed in my trophy room. My most memorable hunt was for polar bear. I hunted for twenty-two straight days in February and March, in the Arctic cold and with only a tent for shelter, challenging broken ice floes. The hunt ended without success, but I returned in May and after eight more days took one of my most prized trophies.

I feel my trophy room is an extension of my hunting adventures, and for me it is full of memories.

CABELA

There is a moment after a successful hunt—after the animal is down, after the pictures have been taken, after the adrenaline has begun to wear off—when you think about the glassing, the tracking, and the stalk. You remember the sounds of birds chattering, the scent of dust mixed within an air so fresh it actually smells peaceful, and you feel certain you will never forget any of it. Yet you realize that all moments tend to fade over time, and you vow to never let them disappear forever.

Those moments, when you can still remember it all, when it seems as if it will last forever—those are the moments we wanted to capture in our trophy room. These animals are not just trophies or fine works of taxidermy and creatures re-created in natural habitat. They are preservations of a part of our lives we can only revisit in our memories. We did not want a room that showcased our hunting adventures—we wanted a room that came alive, a room that could breathe. So we hired the best people we could find, shared our vision, and asked them to bring their own ideas. We gave them a certain freedom to create and explore, and one result of that is a sense that the animals were allowed to roam.

A part of that is placement, but only a small part. The talents of the taxidermists, led by Woodbury, brought these animals to life by setting them in natural poses doing so many of the things we witnessed during those days in the field. The lighting, sound, and special effects, led by the unique talents of the Music Lab team from Austin, Texas, transformed it all into something that moved. Sunsets, constellations, thunderstorms, waterfalls, the sounds of birds and beasts and insects—all of it coalesced to create a sense of adventure. Our room is like a guide who, though not required, can help enhance the experience, much like a hunting expedition to an unfamiliar land.

For us, our trophy room is a reflection of the need to explore—the same need that pushed us out into the prairies and hills when we were children, staring out into a world that held only wonder and awe and hope. If we had known what was beyond that next hill, if we had known the direction our lives would turn, if we had known how our own children would turn out, if we had known ahead of time of the contradictions of life—pain to satisfaction, pleasure to regret, patience to peace, and that the worth of a person has no outside measurement—our lives may have turned out differently. If we had known, would there have been a reason to climb to the top of the mountain, to follow the single set of tracks into the thornbush, or to hike with open hearts toward the sunset? The answer is yes.

If we could see tomorrow, life would hold no adventure.

CHATEAU DE GIEN

Europe's hunting tradition has produced a large number of castles and estates that were later converted to museums devoted to the traditions of the chase. Especially in Germany and France, these museums exist in numbers. They display a rich heritage and often follow the historical evolution of hunting over hundreds of years.

One particularly nice example is Chateau de Gien, which is located in the Loire Valley, traditionally the place where French nobility had its country estates throughout the ages. It is all the more interesting in that it houses general historical hunting artifacts as well as specific trophy collections from French hunters. The chateau is an imposing building with high walls and a slate roof with a steep incline and multiple turrets.

The museum was founded in 1952, and more than 20,000 people visit it each year. The origins of the building date back to medieval times, and it was none other than Joan of Arc who stayed there during her campaigns in support of the French king. In the Renaissance, Anne de Beuajeu, countess of Gien, had the house completely transformed, taking it from a medieval castle to a residence with vast windows and, thereby, permanently abandoning its military functions of the past.

The multiple rooms devoted to hunting are arranged in a chronological manner with the first four rooms covering the period of the sixteenth through the nineteenth centuries. Beautiful antique weapons and crossbows are on display as well as trophies well over a hundred years old. One of the many large paintings reminds us that Louis XI in 1467 deployed a corps of wolf hunters to protect the royal game. There is also on display one of the last wolves shot in the region. Walking through these rooms, the visitor gets a perfect picture of the evolution of firearms from wheel-lock guns to flintlocks, to breechloaders, and eventually the hammerless gun. Numerous decorative works of art in ceramic, tapestry, glass, as well as costumes and hunting accessories are to be seen. In addition, there are rooms devoted to early traps, falconry, and paintings.

The museum has the largest collection of buttons from livery of the huntsmen—those who partook in the chase after deer with horse hounds. Over four thousand buttons are on display including very rare ones from Louis XIV's hunting livery and one with an effigy of Joan of Arc.

The museum houses the trophy collections of Claude Hettier de Boislambert, who was president of the CIC, and Françoise de Grossouvre, chairman of presidential hunts in France. Each collection is on display in a separate room, and the collections feature African, European, and Asian trophies as well as modern firearms.

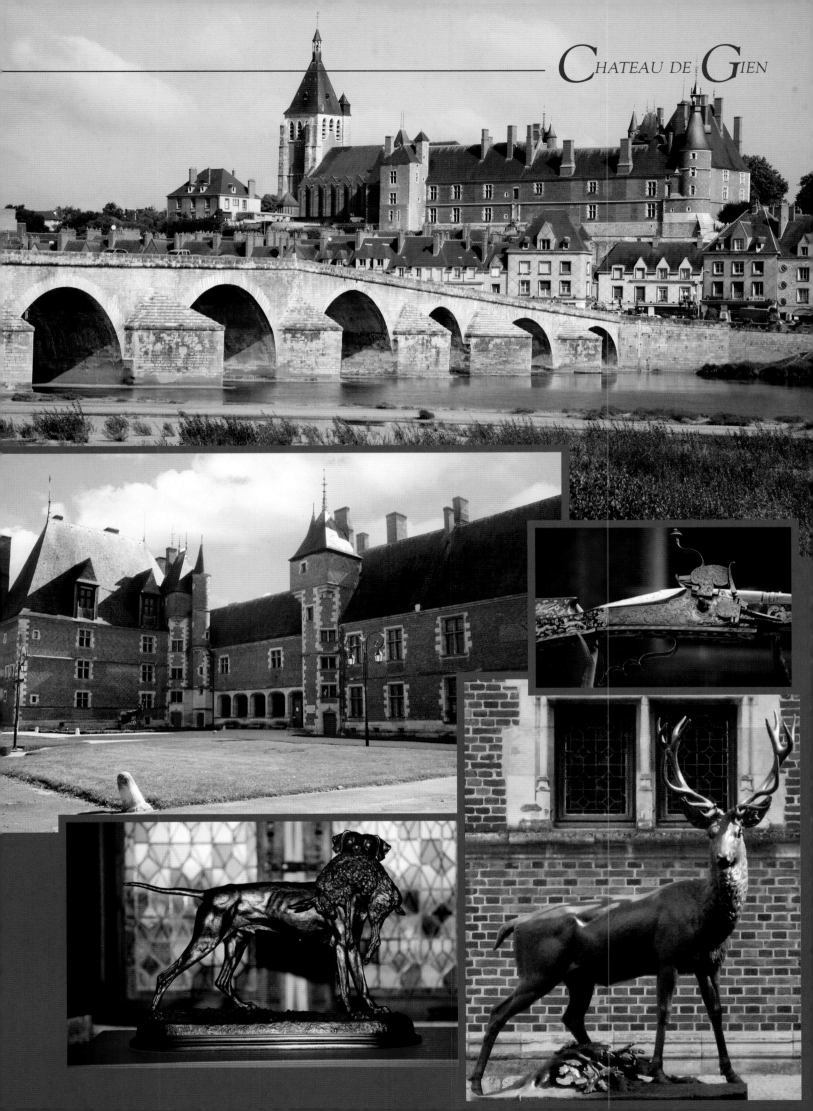

CHATEAU DE GIEN

D'AOUST

As a child, I was fascinated by the beauty and behavior of wild animals. All my free time was spent fishing, trapping, and hunting, mainly for raccoons, ground hogs, squirrels, frogs, turtles, and weasels. I trapped golden finches (canaries) and raised some, and I also kept groundhogs in a pen. I was bitten when I was twelve and almost lost a finger. I might as well have lost it then because I lost that same finger six months ago at the age of seventy-four! In my high school yearbook when I was in the eleventh grade, the students nominated me as the most likely to one day own a zoo.

Between the age of sixteen and twenty-two, I quit hunting and fishing and devoted all my time in the pursuit of the fair sex. I thought women were the most beautiful of god's creatures. I still think the same way. From that age until I was thirty, I didn't hunt because I was busy building a business, paying off mortgages, and raising a family, but I managed some fishing trips with my dad.

When I was thirty-four, I booked a caribou hunt in northern Quebec. I was hooked. From then on I became addicted to the chase and began hunting all types of game. The following year I hunted black bear, moose, and elk in British Columbia, the year after that I hunted sheep and goat; and then I hunted Dall sheep in the Mackenzie Mountains and Yukon moose in the same area. I hunted sheep and pronghorn in Alberta, Canada.

In 1978, I went to Zambia and obtained twenty-five trophies. I fell in love with Africa. I may point out that I was the last sport hunter to obtain a license for a black rhino. Since then, I have been to Africa thirty-four times, namely South Africa, Namibia, Zimbabwe, Tanzania, the C.A.R., Cameroon, Ethiopia, Botswana, Liberia, and Mozambique. I also hunted in the U.S.A., Pakistan, Tajikistan, Azerbaijan, Turkey, Kazakhstan, Argentina, Paraguay, Mexico, Australia, New Zealand, New Caledonia, Spain, the Czech Republic, England, Iran, Ireland, and Newfoundland.

In 1981, I moved to Iqaluit, Nunavut. I worked in the Arctic for twenty-two years. In 1995, I was the first nonresident to obtain a permit for a walrus. Canada North Outfitting organized this trip for me—many thanks to Jerome and Halina Knap.

Hunting is a fascinating sport. You meet fine people, make friends, and, most importantly, contribute to the protection and proliferation of game. We true sport hunters have in the past and in the future will do more than any other group for the welfare and protection of wildlife everywhere.

The students were close when they predicted I'd one day own a zoo. I do not own a zoo, per se, but I have a fair collection of trophy animals and fish!

Good hunting to all. Enjoy your sport. Life is short.

DICKSON

    Mark Dickson, a native of Southern California, is very passionate about a few things in life. In this order it appears to be his family, his business, hunting, and traveling. Hunting has been a part of Mark's family's life from a very young age. His grandparents emigrated from Scotland to Iowa, where his grandfather became a coal miner. In order to survive, he provided food for his family by hunting and fishing. The tradition of hunting was passed down through the generations, and when Mark was nine, his father gave him a pellet gun. During Mark's childhood, his father inspired him to be passionate about the hunt by taking him on various hunting and fishing trips.

    Mark is currently the president of his family-owned business, Astro Aluminum Treating Company, which is a commercial treater of aluminum alloys for most every major aircraft and aerospace programs. He is very fortunate to have created an exceptional group of people who have worked together as a team for over thirty years. While he remains very involved in his business, the trust he has in his staff has allowed him the freedom to pursue what has become a passion for his entire family: big-game hunting and traveling throughout the world and experiencing different cultures together.

    It was his close friend, David Combes, who introduced Mark to the thrill of big-game hunting. Mark and his wife, Janice, had been very involved in supporting their daughters, Lauren and Melissa, in the sport of volleyball. Soon after the girls graduated, they realized that they had a lot more free time on their hands, and Mark decided to give big-game hunting a try. He became immediately hooked, and soon after introduced Janice and his son, William, to the sport as well. It soon became an important part of their life.

    To date Mark and his family have gone on hunting trips to Texas, Canada, Mexico, Argentina, Scotland, New Zealand, Mongolia, Mozambique, South Africa, Botswana, and Alaska. He and William have hunted nilgai, white-tailed and Coues deer, turkey, ducks, dove, wolf, Cape buffalo, sable, oryx, Livingstone eland, blue and black wildebeest, bushbuck, impala, nyala, kudu, warthog, bushpig, and most recently, elephant.

    One of Mark's most memorable trips was hunting roe deer at Balmoral Castle in Scotland. Most exceptionally, Mark holds the world record for a red stag that scored 640, which he shot in New Zealand in May 2011. Thus far he is especially proud of his collection of four North American wild sheep (FNAWS) that include Dall, Stone, desert bighorn, and Rocky Mountain. In addition he has collected red, Armenian, aoudad, and Hangai argali sheep.

    Four years ago Mark decided that he wanted a place, other than his home, to display the many trophies he had acquired. After finding the right builder, architect, and interior designer, the project of converting an empty warehouse into what would become an amazing gathering place for family and friends was put into place. The original design was taken from a photo of Deyrolle, the 177-year-old taxidermy shop located on the classy Rue du Bac in Paris. Sadly, a year after the trophy room project was started, the famous Deyrolle, and all of its contents, were ruined by fire.

The trophy room project evolved through various phases into what it is today. The feeling in the main trophy room is that of an old English hunting lodge with mahogany wall paneling, moldings, and stone. The wine room takes you back in time as well with the use of reclaimed wood and antique clay floor tiles. The dining room, with its twelve- foot-round African juniper table, has the look of a grand room you might find on an estate somewhere in Montana. A commercial-grade, restaurant-quality kitchen was added, along with an outdoor barbecue area and a beautifully landscaped lawn for outdoor entertaining. The final phase in the project was converting the remaining part of the warehouse into a game room, bar, and restroom area. This was built to look like an outdoor cabin and stone house, and these were made with reclaimed materials—barn wood, stone, and steel roofing. Throughout every phase of the planning, the designers and builders made sure that the trophies were the center of focus, using space and lighting to display each correctly. The many flags of Mark's exploits hang beautifully over the entrance within the warehouse.

Like the owner of Deyrolle in Paris, Mark is a collector of many things. Along with the trophies that gracefully adorn the walls and hallways are many beautifully displayed collections. A collection of new and antique riding spurs fill one side of a lighted mahogany wall cabinet and the other side is filled with prize winning, hand-carved and hand-painted duck decoys. The gun room displays antique guns and intricate knives and the walls look much like an art museum, with many paintings reflecting the landscape and life of places he has traveled. Finally, behind the warehouse is an indoor koi pond where he houses his champion koi collection, many of which have been shown in Japan.

The sport of hunting has impacted the Dickson family on many levels. It has exposed them to many cultures and experiences around the world. It has brought many new friends and craftsmen involved in the sport into their lives. For those friends and family who haven't experienced the sport of hunting or traveling themselves, it has given them a place to see, touch, and feel the animals and the relics gathered from the family's adventures. Holidays, birthdays, and gatherings for friends, employees, and family all happen at the trophy room. Clearly, the Dickson trophy room is a place of exceptional beauty and comfort.

GÓMEZ SEQUEIRA

Dr. Marcial Gómez Sequeira was born in Madrid in 1940 and has been married for over forty-five years to Maria Teresa Cruz-Conde, known amongst friends as Maite. Maite and Marcial have two daughters, Monica and Marta, and three grandchildren, Marcos, Martín, and Mía. Marcial's daughters have not followed in his hunting footsteps, but his grandchildren have accompanied him on various hunting trips and are already becoming his ardent hunting companions.

Although not born into a hunting family, Marcial began his hunting career at an early age, and for more than fifty years he has practiced this incredible sport nonstop and participated in all of its related activities. His studies in medicine and his career as a doctor and entrepreneur precluded Marcial from hunting abroad until 1971 when he first traveled to Angola. Since then, he has been obsessed by the "call of Africa," and has returned to the continent fifty-four times and visited more than fifteen countries, some of which have subsequently closed their doors to hunting.

In 1982, his obsession with mountain hunting (wild sheep and goats) kicked in, and he was awarded his first SCI Grand Slam. Since then he has collected forty species of wild sheep, twenty-nine wild goats, and fourteen wild oxen from around the world. In 1987 he traveled to Australia and New Zealand where in only thirty-one days he was able to collect every species permitted. Shortly after, he spent twenty-one days in North America where he traveled to five areas and collected the last seven animals he lacked from the United States and Canada; his collection now totals sixty species and fifty-five exotics from North America.

Marcial has collected fourteen big elephant trophies, six of which weigh in excess of one hundred pounds. The last elephant Marcial obtained was on his second safari with his daughter Marta, when she was only ten. Since then, he has ceased hunting this wonderful pachyderm, concluding that his elephant tally was already sufficient. In recent years, Marcial has focused on obtaining new, important, and unique trophies like the new No. 1 European mouflon and the top five European red deer, which he hunted recently. He just returned from the Philippines with six new trophies, including a sambar deer, which will likely be the first entry of a new species in the SCI record book.

In order to accommodate his immense collection, Marcial had to enlarge his trophy room on various occasions, but he still could not house all his specimens, for he had collected over 400 species in approximately 500 hunting trips throughout five continents. He finally decided to refurbish an additional area on his Madrid property to house all the Spanish trophies independently. These, alone, totaled approximately 2,000 animals, and among them there are 120 gold, 110 silver, and 122 bronze medals.

Marcial has a great love for wildlife and nature, and has protected, bred, and cared for many red, fallow, and roe deer, mouflon, and wild boar on his properties in Spain. He has equally participated in foundations and initiatives aimed at preserving wildlife and its habitat. His house has always been home

to an immense variety of animals, from birds and dogs, to deer, monkeys, and even a lioness.

Marcial is also an avid writer and has published a total of thirteen books that detail his adventures spanning the five continents; he currently has another book in production. He is planning on publishing future editions in the English language, and is already working on additional stories of past and present hunting experiences.

To date, Marcial's awards and recognitions to his hunting career have been significant and many in number: C&S Hunter of the Year award, all of the SCI Diamond awards, all of the Inner Circle awards within the SCI Diamond categories, the Castilla La Mancha Diana Award, C&S award to the Defense of Wildlife and Nature, Barbón award to the Defense of Wildlife, Fundación Natura Lifetime Achievement award, and so on. Equally important, he has garnered every SCI Grand Slam available, and he has over seventy entries in SCI's record books that place in the top ten. His dynamism and restlessness continue unblemished, and his intention to travel farther around the world to practice this ultimate sport remains as firm as ever.

IRANIAN RED SHEEP

KAUFFMAN

I was born in Pennsylvania, one of eight children. I was the only one to become a hunter. My father and I would fly fish for trout each weekend, all year long. From the time I was fourteen, I would run a trapline every fall. My first trophy was a 3x4 whitetail that I shot with a bow when I was sixteen.

I purchased my first big-game hunt at a Lehigh Valley Safari Club fundraiser when I was twenty-three. My wife, Linda, and I enjoyed a two-week adventure to Alaska to hunt Dall sheep, caribou, and moose. From that trip on I was hooked, and immediately on my return home I found myself planning our next trip.

My first African safari was to Tanzania where I was privileged to hunt with the legendary "Cat Man" Cotton Gordon. I collected forty-four animals on that first safari. On one special day I collected three of the Big Five—a lion, a leopard, and a Cape buffalo. I have since hunted in Africa four times. In addition to Africa, I have hunted the United States, Canada, Russia, Tajikistan, the Arctic, and New Zealand. I have been able to experience a wide variety of hunting and cultures around the world. From baboon to polar bear, each animal is special to me. My favorite trophies are my African Big Five, mountain sheep and goats, Marco Polo sheep, polar bear, and Kodiak brown bears.

My best trips have always been those I spent with friends and family. I have shared many campfires with my wife, Linda; daughter Hope; twin sons Harrison and Hunter; and with our family's friends, the Lucks. A trip is just that much better when you can share it and remember it with the people you love.

I can explain the conservation reasons for why one hunts, but the day my daughter asked me why I hunt I told her, "It just feels right." I love sitting in my tree stand on the HHH Ranch in Montana, reading and enjoying wildlife. I also find much joy in improving the habitat for wildlife. I have learned that half the fun of international big-game hunting is looking forward to the next adventure.

My trophy rooms have always been very important to me. I always purchase the best taxidermy I can. I have many life-size mounts and have always displayed them as naturally as possible. One mount I am very proud of is of a lion, lioness, and two lion cubs. Of course, the cubs died of natural causes, and I was able to purchase the skins to create this special mount. I have mounted as many life-size animals as space would allow so that I could remember the entire animal, and not just the horns or antlers.

I would recommend all hunters join Safari Club International. This organization protects your right to hunt and promotes the conservation of wildlife. SCI will also provide the blueprint for your hunting career.

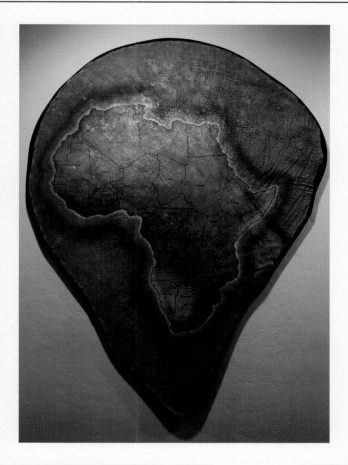

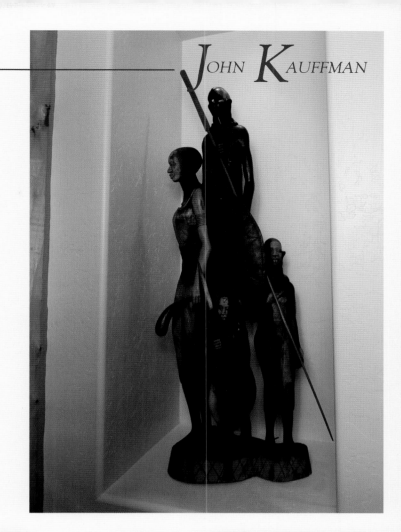

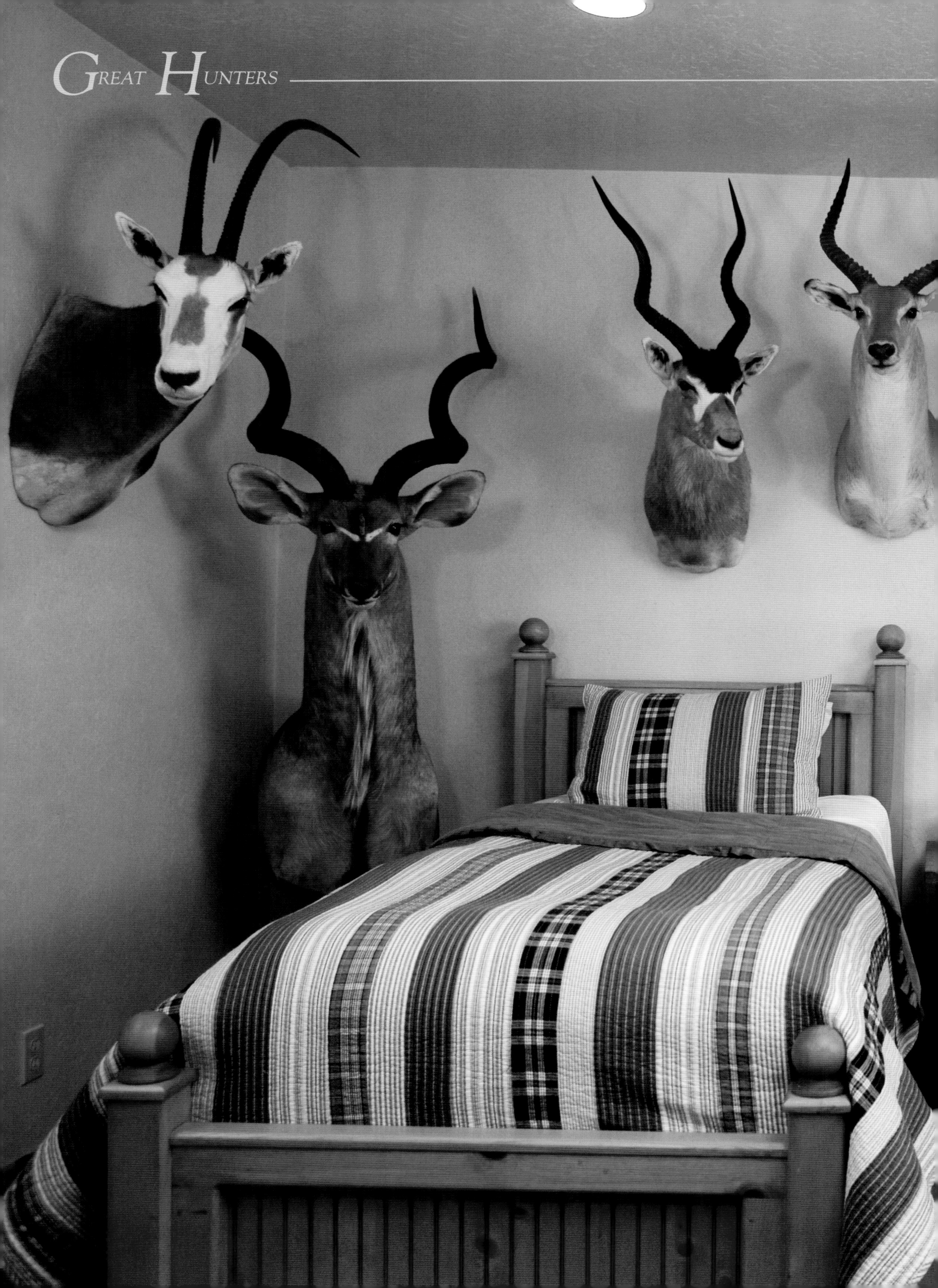

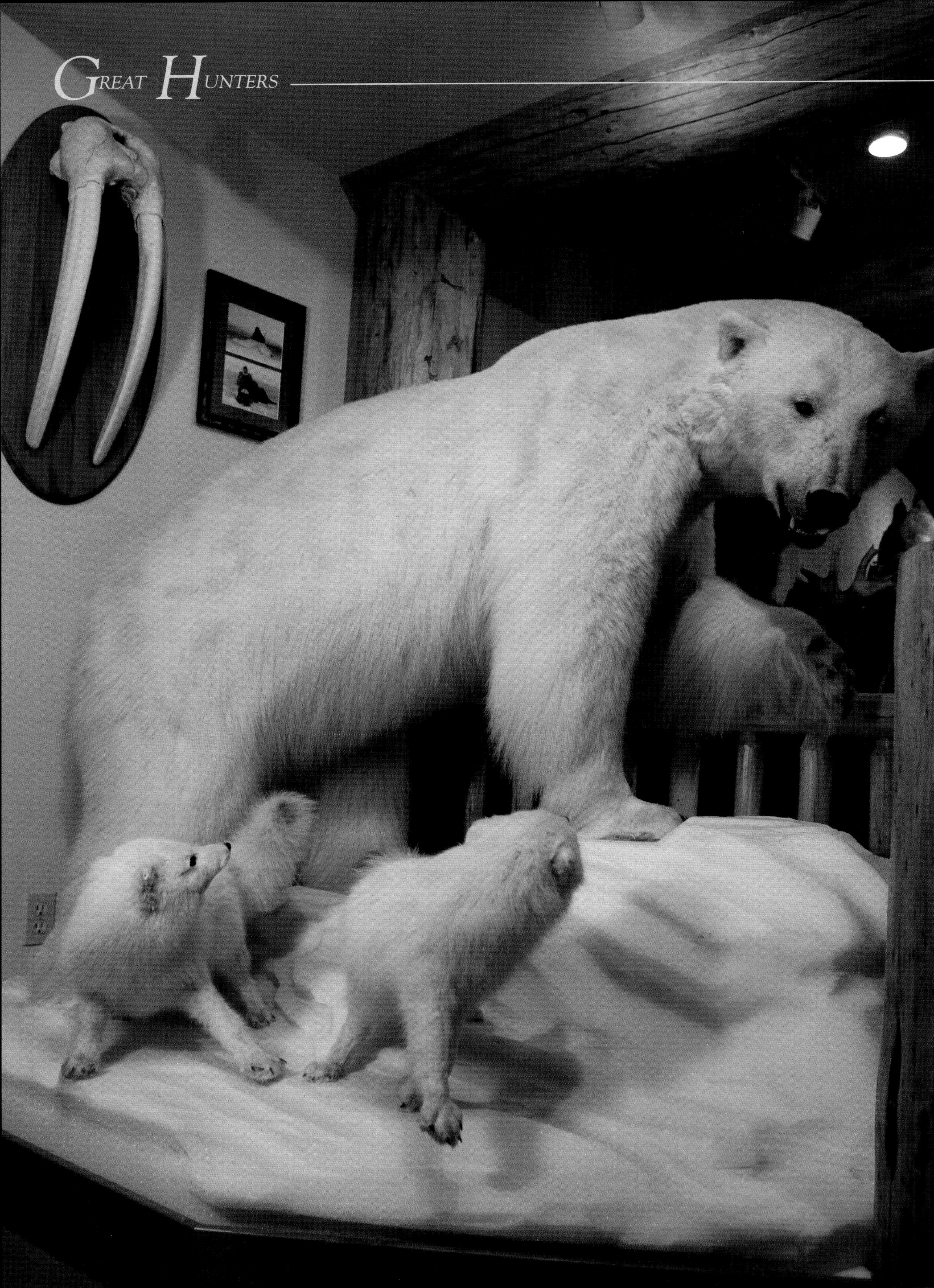

KNAP

Friends and visitors have often remarked that it is not only the trophy room but also our entire house that is a shrine to our many hunts and trips around the world. To some degree that is true. There is not a room in our house that does not have some artwork or artifact from our hunting trips; these range from oil paintings of wildlife and sculptures to shields, spears, and other weapons, and, of course the trophies themselves. Our house represents the totality of forty years of hunting and traveling memories—thirty of which were shared with my wife, Halina.

Halina's office and our library is the home of my collection of turkeys and other birds, and it houses my brown bear with black-powder elk as well. The dining room has a pair of elephant tusks that I shot in the early 1970s in Zambia's Luangwa Valley when I worked for the late Norman Carr's Wilderness Trails. Our trophy room was created in a seldom-used indoor poolroom. The room has an intimate two-tier sitting area where we entertain frequently. My desk overlooks the entire room.

The only major trophy that I don't have in my trophy room or anywhere in my house is my life-size polar bear with a ring seal in its mouth. The polar bear is the symbol and logo of our company, Canada North Outfitting, Inc., which I started in 1980 to outfit and market hunts in the Northwest Territories and Nunavut, Canada. My polar bear is on long-term loan to the Ontario Federation of Anglers and Hunters/Mario Cortellucci Hunting & Fishing Heritage Centre in Peterborough, Ontario.

Because I had been traveling to and hunting in Africa since the early 1970s, in 1981 I started Global Expeditions to market international hunts. Much of Canada North's and Global Expeditions' success must be credited to Halina's support and hard work as the office manager.

Halina and I have enjoyed going to new destinations, such as Siberia in 1995 and 1996, Iran in 1999 and 2000, and Kazakhstan in 2001. We jokingly say that I have taken Halina on two cruises, but both were walrus hunts—one in Nunavut in the Canadian Arctic and one in Russia's north Pacific.

My most memorable souvenir includes a very comfortable chair from the Czech Republic that a forester spent many winter evenings carving out of shed antlers. The forester refused to sell his work until he fell in love and needed money in order to set up a proper house for his bride. I also highly prize the matched set of double narwhal tusks that I bought from one of our hunting guides in Qikitarjuaq, Nunavut. One narwhal out of five hundred tusks has a double tusk, but most of these are uneven in length. A perfectly matched double tusker is very rare.

My trophy room is also an inspiring place in which to return to my first profession as an outdoor writer. Halina and I both plan to do some writing in the future now that Canada North Outfitting is in someone else's capable hands. Far-flung hunts and distant travels will always remain a big part of our future.

"Red Sheep"
December 2006
Temple Guest Reserve
Iran

MAKI

Hunting and the outdoors have defined both my life and professional career. Since I was old enough to hold a .22 rifle growing up in New England, I have been a lifelong hunter. After completing my Ph.D. in wildlife and fisheries management at Michigan State University, I have spent thirty years working on worldwide wildlife and environmental projects for the oil patch. I am now semiretired and devote my time to running the Safari Club International Conservation program. Together with my wife, Ann, we live on our ranch in Alpine, Wyoming, where we are surrounded by the Bridger-Teton and Caribou National Forests within full view of the Wyoming and Salt River Mountain Ranges.

Like most of us, I started hunting with my dad in New Hampshire, progressing from grouse and rabbits to white-tailed deer. As work took us around the country, I had the opportunity to hunt many North American species, and that fired my interest in seeing different places and new animals. I have hunted on six of the seven continents and in most U.S. states and Canadian provinces. While my family and I were residents of Alaska, I served as guide and outfitter for my three sons in their quest to hunt the Alaskan Big Five; those hunts will always be my fondest memories. Now the tradition continues as my grandsons and granddaughters have also become big-game hunters.

Mountain game remains my passion. I have now climbed in all the major mountain ranges of the world, and I have seen many more fabulous vistas than I can possibly recount. I have completed the Grand Slam of Sheep, the World Sheep Slam, the World Capra Slam, and the Triple Slam of Mountain Game. I have been on fifteen African safaris, have taken all the dangerous game, and completed the SCI Crowning Achievement Award. Fishing is also an important pursuit, and the trophy room has a wall dedicated to the big-game fish of the world. Because fly-fishing fills the summer months, I have also completed the Saltwater Fly Fishing Grand Slam.

I designed our log home and imported the logs from British Columbia. They are all hand-scribed Engelmann spruce, ranging up to thirty inches in diameter, and the logs provide a rustic and natural backdrop for the animals. Our trophy room has served as a center for many political and social functions here in western Wyoming. We conduct regular tours for school children, scout troops, and many other local organizations. I feel it is an excellent opportunity for our young people to develop an appreciation for wildlife and the pivotal role that hunting plays in the restoration, management, and conservation of North American game species.

I have always enjoyed history, and so it was a natural extension to become interested in the study and collection of firearms. Through careful research, I have managed to assemble an extensive

collection of U.S. martial long rifles and pistols dating from the American Revolution. I consider it an honor to be the temporary custodian of many of these rare and historical arms.

I am dedicated and passionate about wildlife conservation, and I am working to ensure that both the hunting and nonhunting communities fully understand the importance of hunting to the conservation of wildlife worldwide. If we can spread this understanding, it will help to ensure a healthy and enduring future for sport hunting.

ALAN MAKI

MINX

It was a brisk December morning in 1960 in the hills of eastern Missouri that I bagged my first rabbit while hunting with my grandfather and father. One shot with my grandmother's .22, and I was hooked on hunting. I still have that .22, a prized possession. I still remember the fried rabbit, biscuits, and cream gravy my grandfather made as if he had made them only yesterday. Delicious! At eight years old, this was the beginning of a lifelong adventure and love affair with all things hunting.

My grandfather was a passionate hunter and fisherman, and it was from him that I learned to hunt. Every weekend my dad and I went to visit my grandparents we'd plan a hunting trip with him or a fishing excursion, if it wasn't the hunting season. Rabbits and squirrels were my hunting quarry. Then the progression occurred, as I imagine it does for all hunters: quail, ducks, geese, deer, javelina, Russian boars, bear, elk, and so on. If I wasn't hunting, I was working on planning the next trip to Montana, Texas, British Columbia, Mexico, Argentina, or I simply dreamt of the next hunting adventure. During those "growing up" years, I read about Africa in *Outdoor Life* and other magazines. I watched TV and learned about Africa, whether it was *Marlin Perkins' Wild Kingdom, John Wayne's Hatari!*, or *Curt Gowdy's American Sportsman*. I dreamt of Africa.

Fast forward into the twenty-first century: My law firm became successful, and that made Africa a reality! I've hunted in most of the countries in southern Africa. I'm in pursuit of SCI's trophy animals of Africa, and to date I have collected fifty African trophies, which you'll see on the following pages. My Cape eland ranks No. 3 in SCI's record book; my black rhino rank No. 2 (darted); my Livingstone eland ranks No. 10; and I have many other high-scoring trophies. Each, regardless of rank, has a special story and memory. I also have completed the grand slam of Spanish ibex.

I have chronicled my hunting experiences with my *Safari Adventure Productions* DVD series found at www.safariadventureproductions.com. These include *Safari Adventure Zambia, Safari Adventure Botswana, South Africa, New Mexico, Northern Zambia, Argentina,* and *Spain. Safari Adventure Cameroon,* the *C.A.R.,* and *Tanzania* are on the production horizon.

In an effort to give back, I cofounded the Hunter Proud Foundation whose primary purpose is to produce video programs that promote the conservation through utilization principle, as well as the rights of the hunter. Hunters play an important role in wildlife conservation. We pay more for wildlife conservation than any other organization combined. Conservation Force awarded the Hunter Proud Foundation the prestigious Communications Excellence Award.

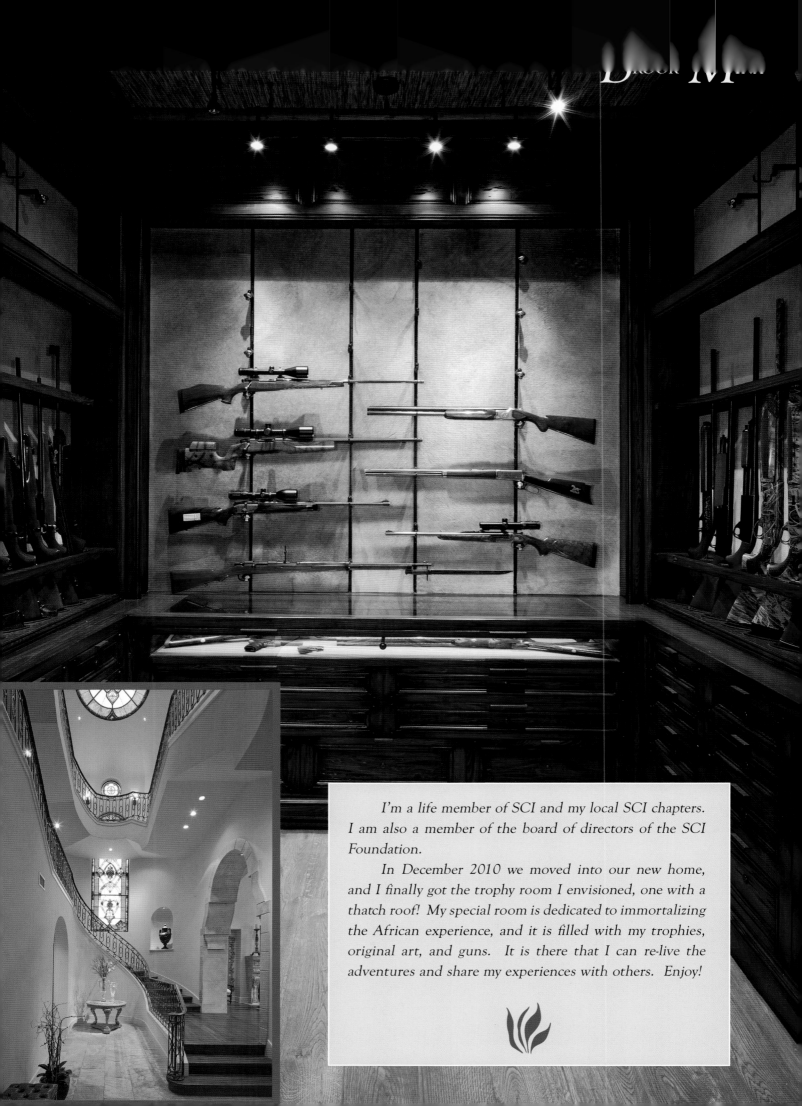

I'm a life member of SCI and my local SCI chapters. I am also a member of the board of directors of the SCI Foundation.

In December 2010 we moved into our new home, and I finally got the trophy room I envisioned, one with a thatch roof! My special room is dedicated to immortalizing the African experience, and it is filled with my trophies, original art, and guns. It is there that I can re-live the adventures and share my experiences with others. Enjoy!

MUSÉE DE LA CHASSE ET DE LA NATURE

 The Musée de la Chasse et de la Nature is a private museum located in the Marais district (3ème arrondissement) of Paris. François Sommer, an industrialist who was passionate about hunting and the protection of wildlife, and his wife, Jacqueline, founded the museum to look after their collection of paintings, tapestries, sculpture, hunting equipment, taxidermy, and other hunting-related objects. The dog room mixes seventeenth-century canine portraits of Louis XIV's pets, a recent Jeff Koons puppy sculpture, and animal collars throughout the centuries in an homage to man's best friend. There's a curiosity cabinet-size room dedicated to the unicorn, and another to the wild boar. The museum is operated by a foundation and is housed in the Hôtel de Guénégaud (1651–1655), designed by architect François Mansart, and since 2002 in the Hôtel de Mongelas (1703) as well. The two houses contain the following collections:

 The Hôtel de Guénégaud features hunting weapons, including crossbows and harquebuses. In addition to a Regency-style room with a sculpture by Jean-Baptiste-Siméon Chardin, there are many hunting-related works of art by Jean-Baptiste-Camille Corot, Alexandre-Gabriel Decamps, Alfred de Dreux, Alexandre-François Desportes, Jean-Baptiste Huet, Jean-Baptiste Santerre, and Antoine Charles Horace Vernet.

 The Hôtel de Mongelas contains taxidermy and trophies; a cabinet of curiosities; and exhibits of birds, wolves, horses, and dogs. Artwork is by Jan Brueghel, Lucas Cranach, André Derain, and Peter Paul Rubens.

 The main collection of trophies is the result of two donations made in 1961 and 1964 by François and Jacqueline Sommer. These donations come in particular from trophies taken by the couple and their friends on the Sommer's estate of Belval in the French Ardennes. There are also trophies brought back from their great hunting trips throughout the world. The Sommers enjoyed hunting in Iran and Alaska, but they had a very particular affection for Africa where they very often traveled and hunted.

 François Sommer (1904–1963) discovered Africa at the height of the colonial era. His childhood in the French Ardennes developed in him a major taste for nature as well as adventure. When he was twenty-five years old, he left on foot and without a guide for his first African safari, which lasted six months. It was the beginning of a long love story with the African continent. In 1934, he crossed Africa on a private plane.

 Sommer denounced the outrageous mechanization of modern safaris and the rarefaction of certain species. According to him, the future of hunting will only be assured through a rigorous management of

wildlife. He tried to make African leaders understand the need for conservation. Concerned with the dangers that confront big game, François Sommer militated for the creation of territories of "controlled hunting" or natural reserves. It was through his intervention that Manda, in Chad, became a national park. In France, his friend President Georges Pompidou entrusted him with setting up a hunting estate at Chambord. It was there that a population of stags from Sommer's estate of Belval were reintroduced.

After WWII his wife, Jacqueline (1913–1993), accompanied him in his hunting adventures throughout the world. In time, their equipment in the African bush changed from rifles to cameras. Without forsaking the "traditional" practice of big-game hunting, they instead became hunters of wildlife images.

The Sommers distributed their trophy collection in three rooms; there is a room for African trophies and paraphernalia (most important), a room for the Americas, and a room for trophies from Asia. Along with the trophies, there are weapons and works of art that originate from these areas. The trophies from Europe were distributed in the other rooms of the museum and the other residences managed by the foundation (living rooms of the club, Chambord as from 1971, and Belval as from 1973). After two years of work, the Museum of Hunting and Nature of Paris reopened its doors to the public in 2007.

Today, the museum maintains more than 550 hunting trophies at the Paris and Chambord residences. In addition, the trophies from the estate at Belval include more than 150 species. The trophies in these collections have been donated by eighty individuals and families. In geographical proportion: America 6 percent; Asia 14 percent; Africa 34 percent; and Europe 50 percent. As of this writing, the foundation is on the point of acquiring the most important donation of its history: the collection of Prince Rodrigue d'Arenberg, which has been offered by his widow. This collection includes several hundred animals from throughout the world.

The Musée de la Chasse et de la Nature is open daily except Mondays and holidays, and an admission fee is charged. (62, rue des Archives, Paris 3éme, France)

REVELLE

Jack Revelle believed in living his life with extreme intensity. Accompanied by Joyce, his wife and beloved companion for fifty-five years, he traveled the globe, from the mountains of Mongolia to the deserts and rain forests of Africa to the frozen tundras of Alaska to the tropical seas of Micronesia.

Jack was an introspective man with a great love for the natural world. He kept poetic journals detailing his many journeys and expeditions. He wrote, "Life consists of a series of experiences" and "in order to create good memories, one must dream big, make daring plans, and execute what one imagines." In addition to being a man of action, Jack was also a risk-taker, in business and in every other aspect of life.

As a young athlete growing up on the outskirts of Chicago, Jack excelled in competitive diving and swimming and became a national champion; he played minor-league football; and he went to Syracuse University on a track scholarship. He tried out for the 1948 Olympics, and a year later set SU's high-jump record of 6 feet, 5½ inches, a record that was not broken for sixteen years!

This man of action had many passions: skiing, scuba diving, motorcycling, skydiving, flying all over the world with Joyce in their Bonanza, but hunting was how he most loved to spend his days. When he was struggling to go to college while supporting his young family, he hunted deer near his upstate New York home to put meat on the table. Later, as the automobile businesses he started gave him the means, he hunted all over the world: from coast to coast in the United States and Alaska, in Mexico, New Zealand, British Columbia, and Mongolia, to name a few. Most precious to him were his adventures hunting on the great African continent where he went ten times with Joyce to Zambia, the Congo, South Africa, and Tanzania.

In his seventy-fourth year, even though they knew he was gravely ill, he and Joyce went on their last African hunt for a trophy Cape buffalo. On the folder where he kept track of all the plans for the upcoming trip, he wrote "PLEASE GOD, ONE MORE TIME." His prayers were answered, and he was able to add a final chapter to his extensive detailed hunting journals.

Jack died in 2001, and he left a collection of over 200 trophy mounts, some 130 species, among them a world record grizzly bear, jaguars, lions, leopards, and a Cape buffalo.

Joyce Revelle donated his journals, along with hundreds of photos, many hours of video, and his huge trophy mount collection to a nonprofit offshoot of Bass Pro Shops. They will soon be on display in a "Wonders of Wildlife" hunting museum in the new Buffalo, New York, Bass Pro store. This collection is a testimony to Jack's belief that life should be lived, whenever possible, as "high adventure." On his nightstand Jack kept a small stone with the message "Live your dreams!" emblazoned on it. On the other side in his unmistakable handwriting, Jack wrote the words: "I have!"

GREAT HUNTERS

SIMPSON

Mike Simpson started hunting with his father in East Texas for squirrels and deer at the age of eight and dreamed of traveling the world to hunt big game as he grew older. He mounted a squirrel for an eighth-grade science project, which set the stage for his life's work.

He attended the University of Houston to become an engineer, but taxidermy and hunting enticed him to forget office work and spend a life in the outdoors. He founded Conroe Taxidermy over forty-eight years ago. Taxidermy opened many opportunities for hunting big game around the world.

With his wife, Becky, Mike made his first African safari to Kenya in 1974, guided by the famous Finn Aagaard. Many trips to Africa followed, and his travels on that continent took him from the Sahara to the Cape. In 1977 Mike journeyed to the High Altai of Mongolia for his first Asian sheep. After completing his Grand Slam at twenty-seven years of age, he continued to hunt to the very far corners of six of the seven continents. Mike became a member of SCI in 1972 and in 1977 he helped put the first record book together; from those roots Mike went on to become SCI's twenty-eighth president in 2005.

Mike won the 2003 Weatherby Award with 274 species; he has won every major SCI award for service and hunting. Mike's boyhood dreams have become a reality as you can see by his new 8,200-square-foot ranch house, which was built on his exotic ranch in Texas. Mike and Becky raised their three sons to become outdoorsmen, and this is a tradition that has been passed on to their grandchildren.

Mike Simpson says, "I cannot even begin to count the numerous memories our trophies and trophy room have evoked for my wife and me, and sharing those memories with our many friends and family has been very rewarding."

STROMBERG

My hunting career started at the age of twelve. My father had just passed away and one of his good friends asked me if I would like to work on his farm. The farm was located in the foot of the Cascade Mountain Range in Washington State. He had four boys, so I fit right in. After chores and working in the berry fields, we would go hunting and/or fishing about every day. That first fall we went deer hunting. I was fortunate to harvest a black-tailed deer and a black bear. To this day I still have my first deer, bear, crow, and squirrel in my trophy-room office.

As my trophy collection grew and hunting adventures took me all over the world, I felt it was time to design a trophy-room-cum-museum. I read articles on what to do and the mistakes to avoid. I determined the following needed to be incorporated into the overall design: The building must be separate from the house, and the structure had to be multi-purpose and not an irregular building, in case something happened to me. Because of insects in our climate, the temperature had to be controlled between 60–70 degrees; likewise I wanted to be able to control the lighting—I wanted easy access to change the direction of lights and the bulbs. I wanted to include an area for a bar, an office, and a maintenance/security room with an alarm system. I wanted the high white walls to be backed by 2"x6" wall construction with a ¾" plywood/sheet rock overlay. I would use zebra wood for the handrails, Australian cypress for the wood floors, and 650-year-old Douglas fir for the front doors, which would be 6 feet wide by 9 feet high. The building would have 4,000 square feet with a second level and walkways. Never did I ever dream that I would fill up the entire building, but, like most trophy hunters, it happened sooner than I could have imagined.

I wanted to vary the groupings of the animals by region, type, and/or country. As the collection grew, that became somewhat more difficult. The trophy room houses over five hundred-plus animals, birds, and fish. I have used many taxidermists throughout my hunting career. Currently, I use Cory Wright Taxidermy and Mike Valentine of Frontier Taxidermy.

For variety, the museum is also home to dozens of bronzes, paintings, and artifacts. There is a 300-piece knife collection; 400-plus books, and 500-plus masks. Some of the more unusual pieces are antique swords, a suit of armor, and a 100,000-year-old Romanian cave bear. One of my hobbies is designing frontier clothing and jewelry, so that is reflected in my trophy room, too.

Many people have viewed my trophy room, and some were nonhunters. They have all said pretty much the same thing: that they were comfortable being in the room because there is so much to look at, other than animals. I always take the opportunity to explain to people why sportsmen are the ultimate conservationists. I say that we must accept our role as conservationists because we have

DOUG STROMBERG

a responsibility as the highest evolved mammal on the planet.

All my adventures have made lasting memories, and they have only been possible through a team effort of professional hunters, trackers, camp staff, and myself. I have hundreds of awards by SCI, and I look forward to many adventures ahead. Through all of this, one person has had great patience with my hunting and collecting, and that would be my wife of forty years, Sandi Stromberg.

Good Hunting!

BLUE DUIKER
BAMINGUI, CENTRAL AFRICAN REPUBLIC

YELLOW BACKED DUIKER
BAMINGUI, CENTRAL AFRICAN REPUBLIC

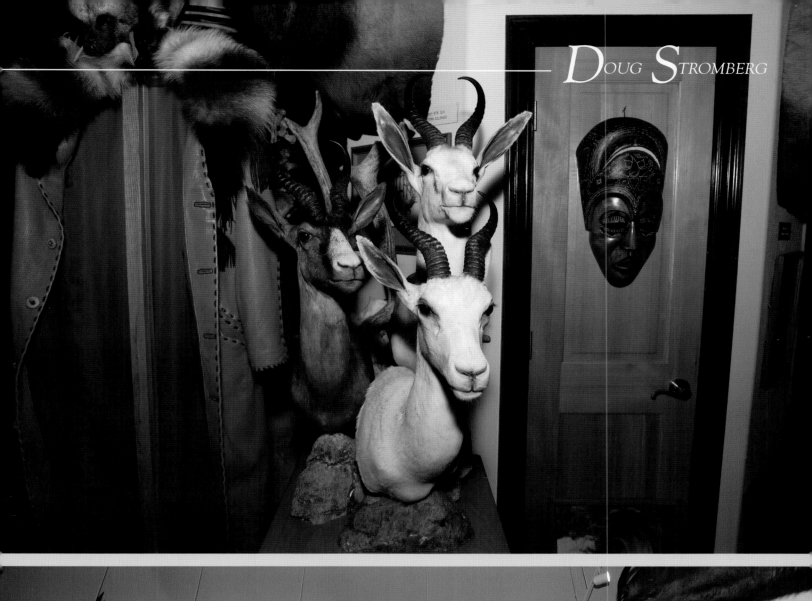

CAVE BEAR - ROMANIA
300,000 - 10,000
YEARS AGO

GREAT HUNTERS

GENET
EASTERN CAPE, AFR

WILLIAMSON

I was born in Fort Worth, Texas, in 1966. As far back as I can remember I have lived my life in the great outdoors. I was very fortunate that my family owns ranches in several parts of the country. This gave me the opportunity to hunt and fish from a very early age.

I remember as a child my family would get together to watch my grandfather's reel-to-reel movies of his hunts in Tanganyika, or Tanzania as it is called today. I knew then that big safaris and Africa would be my passion and calling. While growing up, I would hunt just about everything that was available. I would love to skin and tan my own harvests. This later on in life would make me more responsible toward wildlife and wildlife conservation; and in the end it would enable me to teach my children, other children, and friends about these issues.

My wife, Kasi, and I have three children—Gregory Jr., Elle, and Sawyer—and we are pleased that they also enjoy hunting, fishing, and the great outdoors. It makes me proud to be able to pass along this great tradition that we share and enjoy as a family. They have all collected several species from several continents as well.

I have been fortunate enough to take more than two hundred species from five continents. I have mounted approximately three hundred animals life size, and I have distributed these full mounts among our three homes. I enjoy sharing these trophies with family and friends, and now with this book I have the opportunity to share my trophies with the world.

GREAT HUNTERS

WULFF

The beginnings of the Wulff Jagdmuseum (hunting museum) were found in the private trophy collection of its namesake, Günter Wulff, who housed his trophies originally in a private house in the village of Oerrel, south of Hamburg, Germany. The Wulff Hunting Museum is one of Europe's largest private trophy collections and is today open to the public.

Günter Wulff was born in 1912 and orphaned at the early age of thirteen. Without any immediate family to help, it wasn't until after World War II that he was able to go into business for himself. With a loan of five hundred marks, he began manufacturing slot machines. His business took off and was so successful that he was able to realize his long-held dream to hunt big game. His hunting career began in the 1960s, and once he sold his business in 1972, his hunting activities accelerated.

Günter Wulff had a large gun collection, but his special love was for fine hand-built guns from the small Austrian village of Ferlach. He hunted with a relentless passion and energy, and as his head gamekeeper Albert Meyer recalls, "He would come back from Alaska in the morning and was hunting red stags in the evening on his lease near Oerrel." Despite having hunted in North America, Africa, and Eastern Europe extensively, he loved hunting roe deer on his local property more than anything else.

The hunting museum is over 600 cubic meters (about 21,200 cubic feet) and has two floors; it contains over 700 trophies and mounts. Initially the trophies were simply delivered to the villa and hung anywhere, but over time Günter Wulff decided to bring order to the collection, and so he organized the mounts according to the continent of their origin. He also started working on the enlargement of the villa. In the late 1970s he made the villa into a foundation, capitalized its upkeep, and opened it to the public. Günter Wulff died in 1983, but the museum is still open to the public today and is being ably managed by Albert Meyer, his former head gamekeeper, and Mrs. Meyer, Albert's wife. *

*Translated from *Wild und Hund* magazine by L. J. Wurfbain.